4

BONATTI

© Walter Bonatti 1984
English language edition © Victor Gollancz Ltd 1985

First published in Italy 1984 by
Massimo Baldini Editore, Appiano Gentile, Como
under the title magia del Monte Bianco

This edition published 1985 by
Victor Gollancz Ltd, 14 Henrietta Street, London WC2E 8QJ

British Library Cataloguing in Publication Data
Bonatti, Walter
    Magic of Mont Blanc.
    1. Blanc, Mont (France and Italy)—
    Description and travel
    I. Title   II. Magia del Monte Bianco. English
    914.4'49   DC611.M68

ISBN 0-575-03560-9

Art Director Toshihiro Miki

Printed in Italy

magic
of MONT

Translated by
Geoffrey Byrne-Sutton

BLANC

Victor Gollancz Ltd
London · 1985

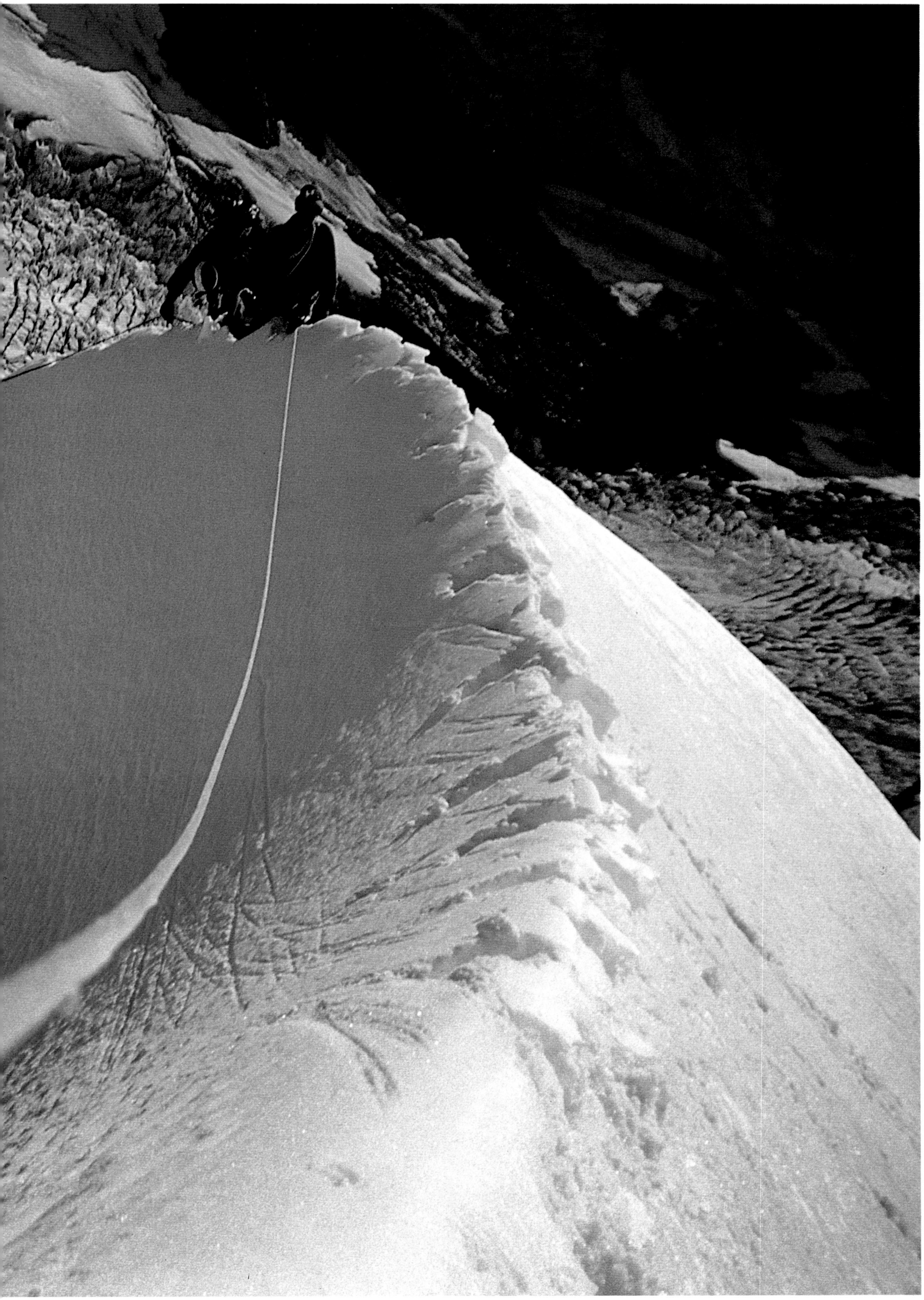

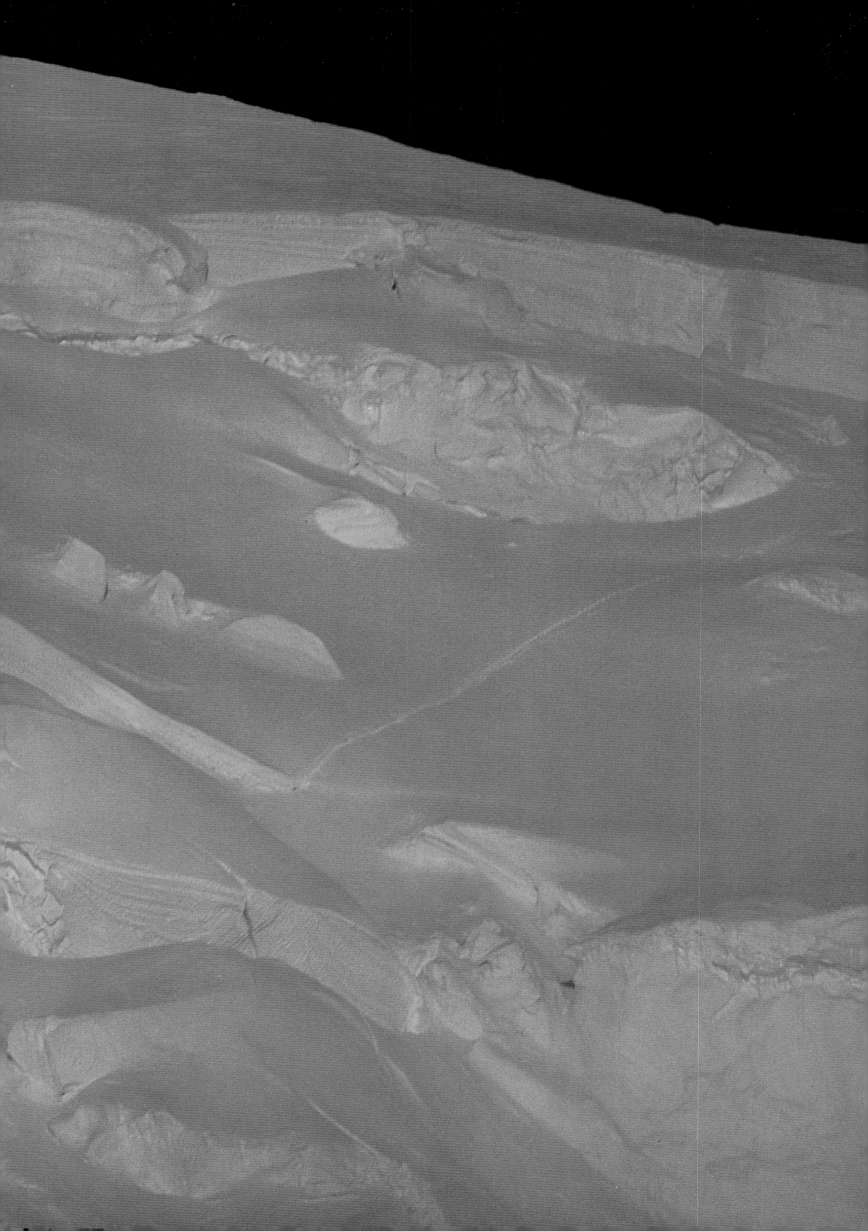

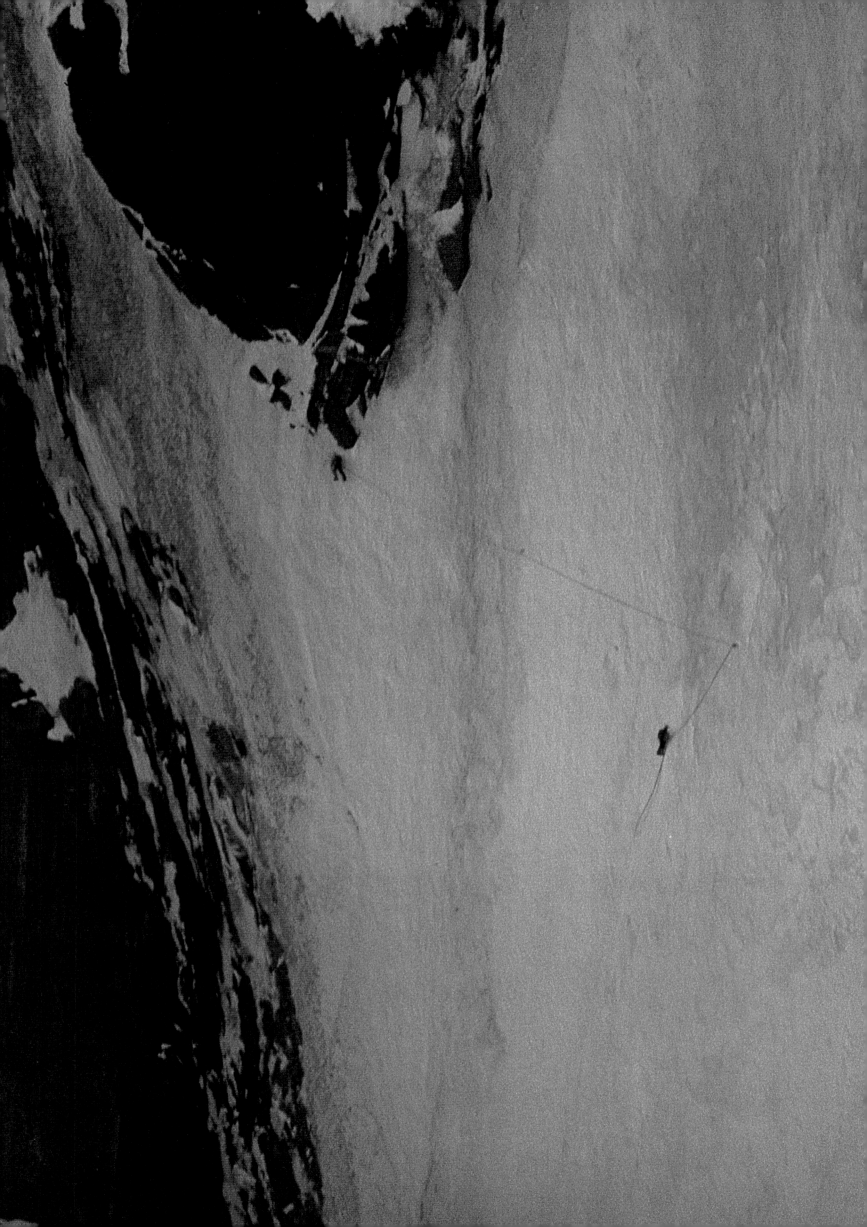

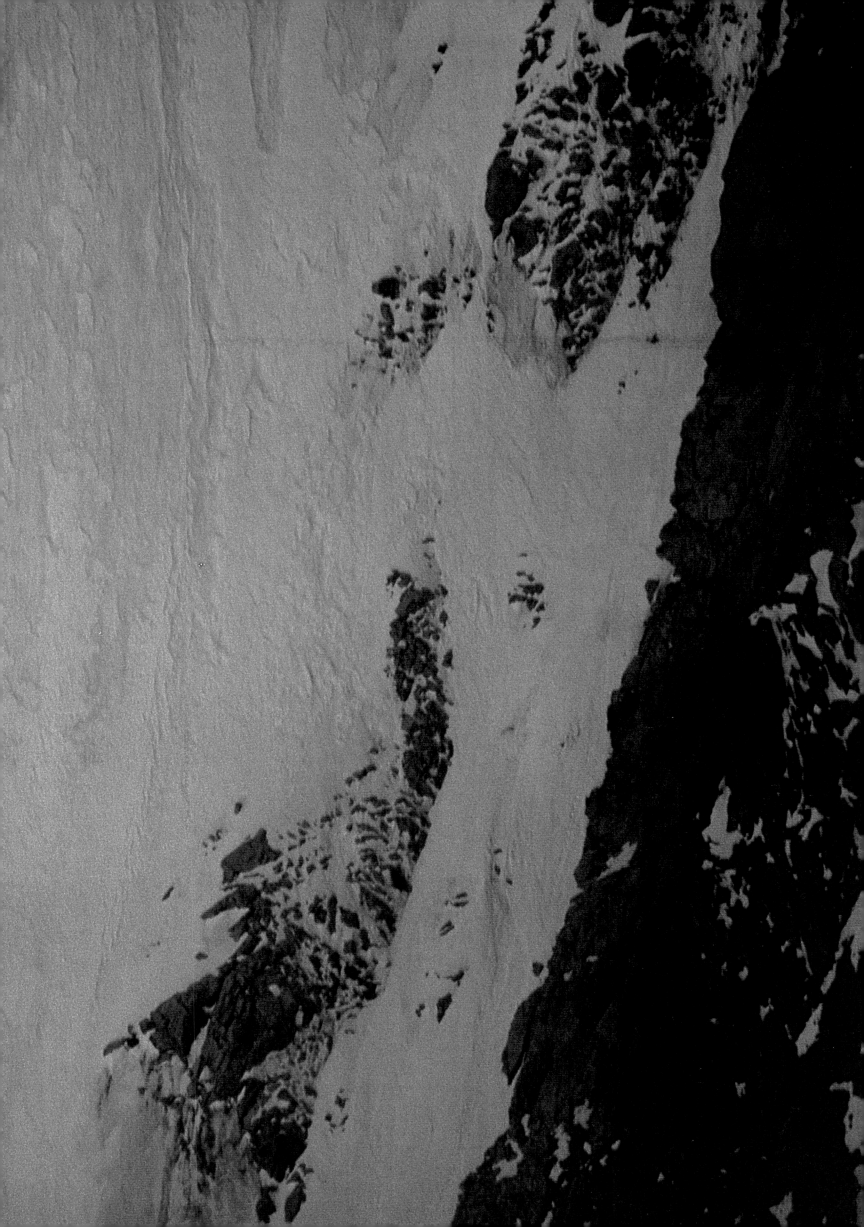

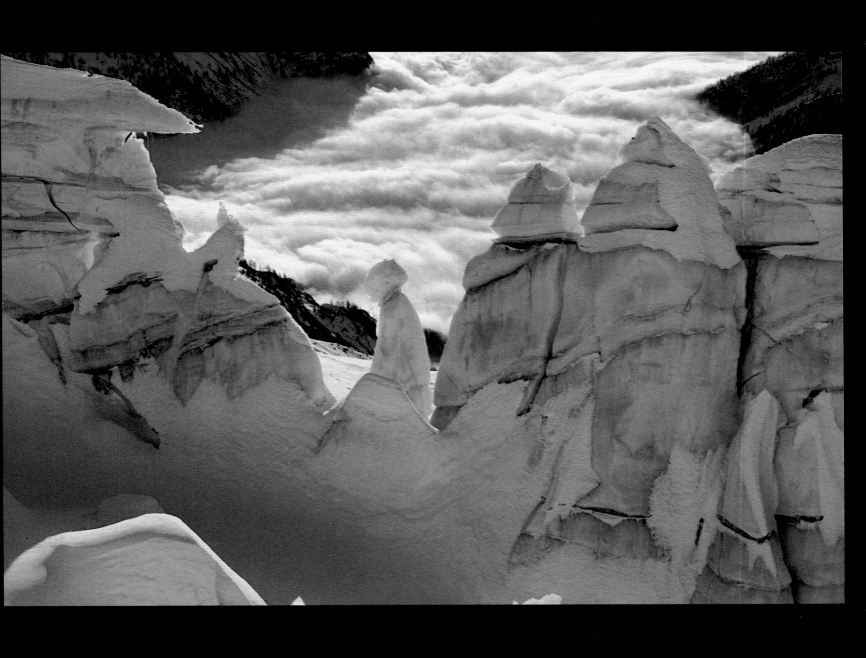

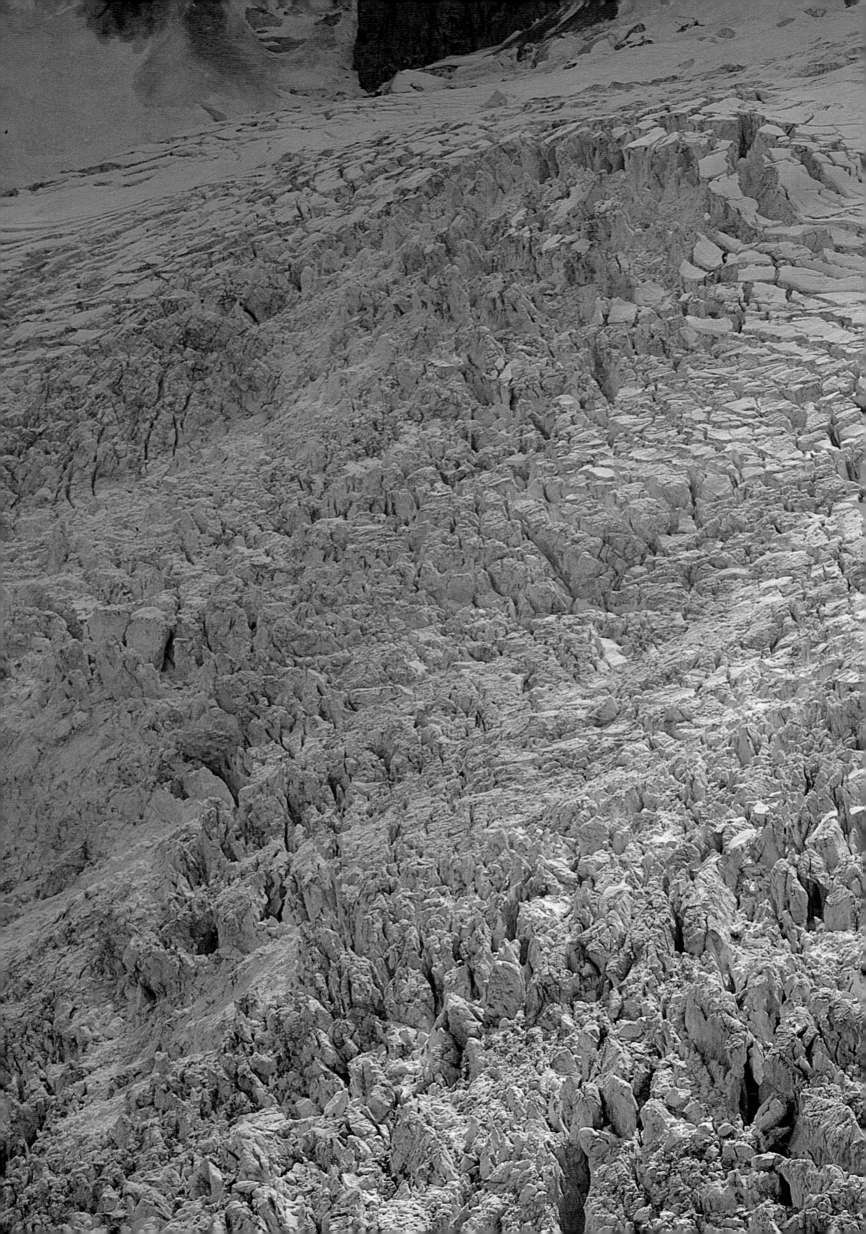

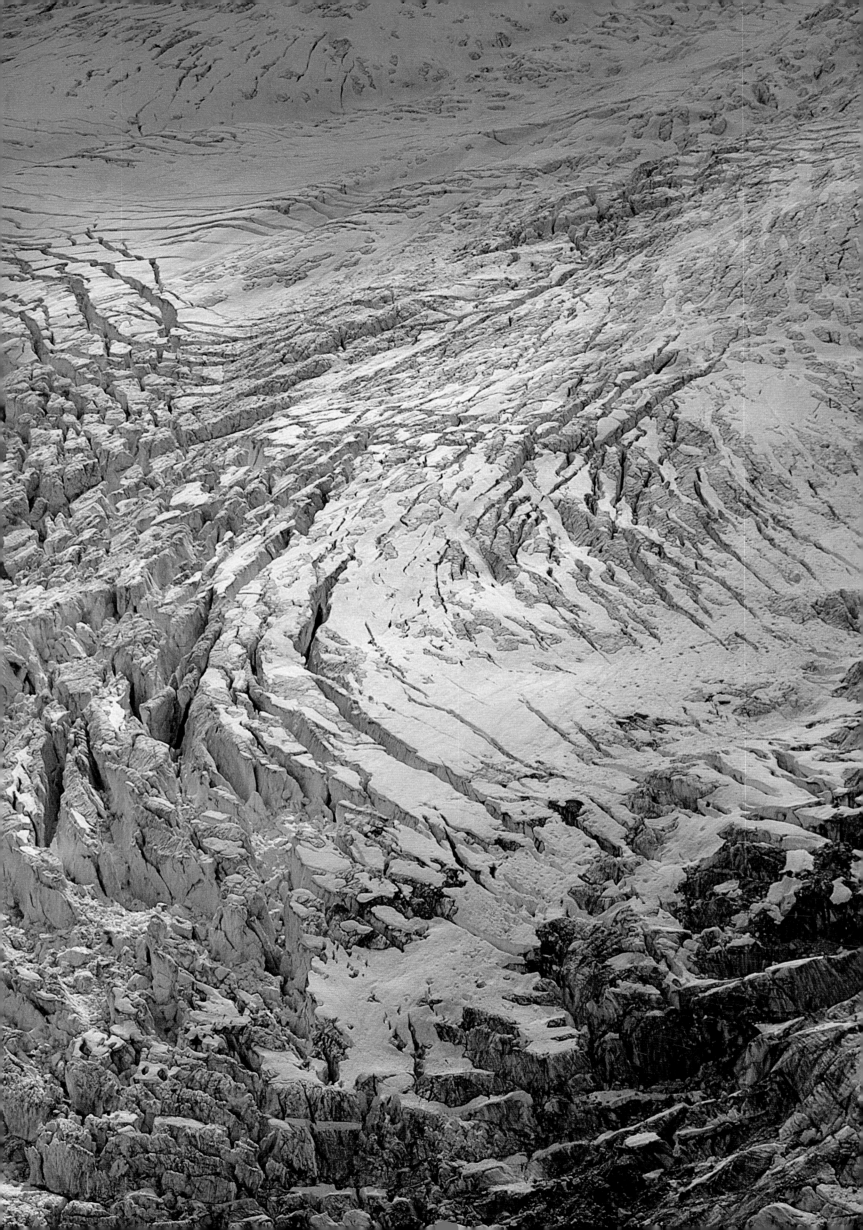

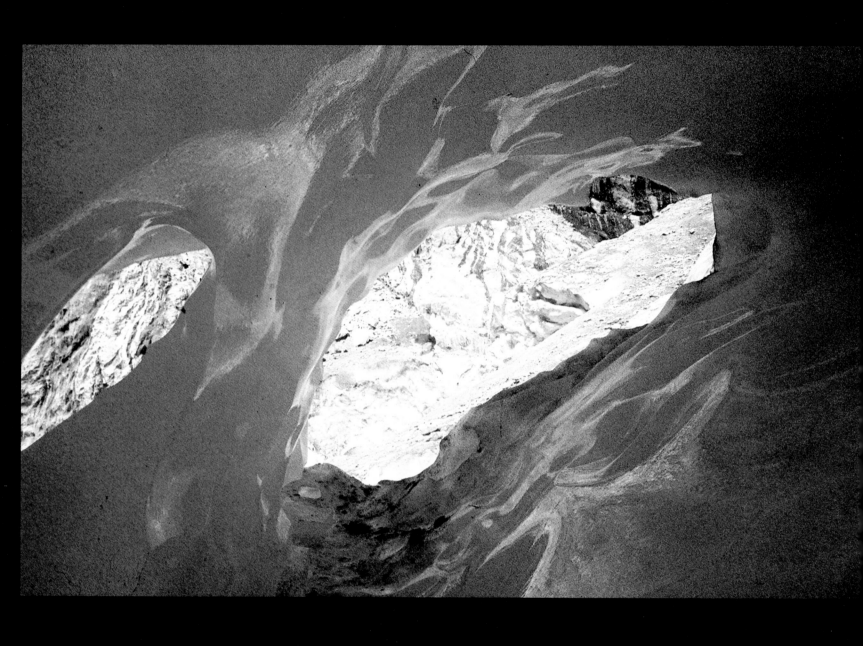

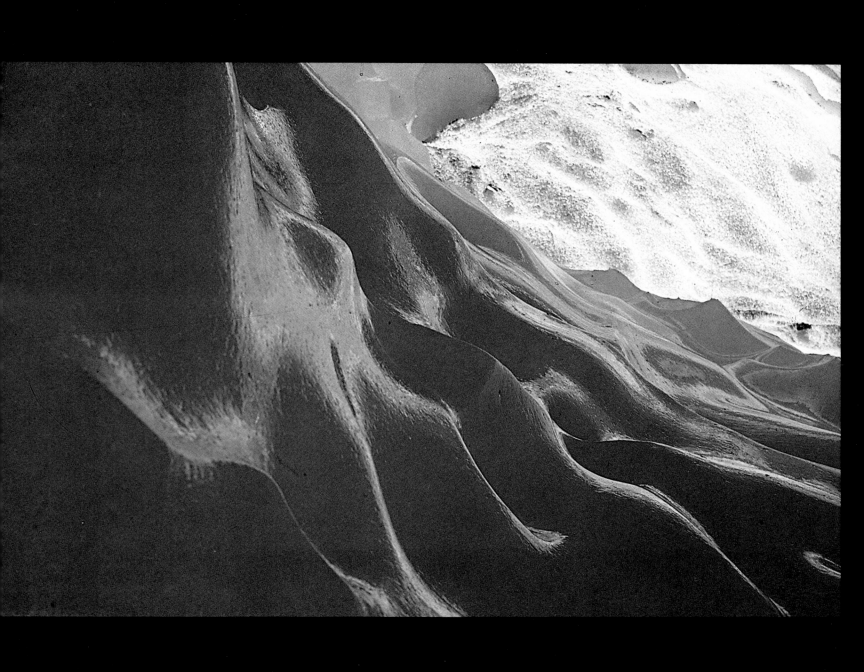

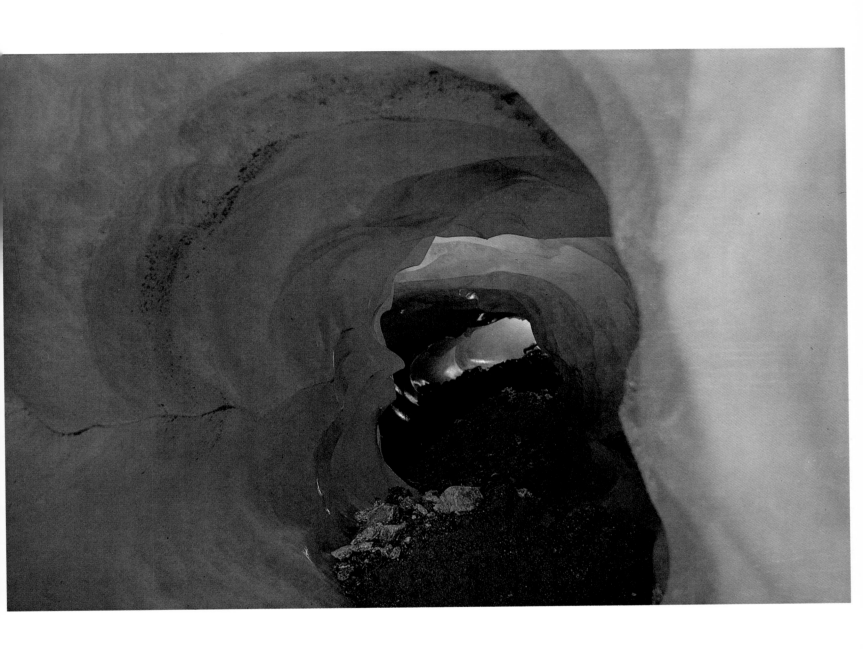

Remembering

It was late afternoon. I was alone, making my way upwards towards the higher regions of Mont Blanc. The slanting rays of late summer set ablaze with vivid colours the last clumps of alpenrose which, intermingled with patches of primula and bellflowers, lent a deceptive feeling of warmth to the landscape, a feeling nevertheless held in check by the many streams of crystal-clear water tumbling from the cold, bare moraines. Thick pine and larch woods climbed some hundreds of metres above the valley floor before dying out on the steep slopes among the colourful patches of willow herb, adenostyles and the bilberry bushes which herald the upper heathland. Among the aromatic odours which rose from below, full of the scent of pines, came frequent earthy smells, dank and clammy, a mixture of rotting fern, fungus and tree-stump. The now numerous ledges were covered in dense cushions of moss campion embroidered with little pink flowers, garnished with thick tufts of house-leek, while in the hollows sprouted the last anemones, glacier crowfoot, sparse dianthus and a hundred other tiny flowers with quaint names and bright colours. Often the hummocks were dotted with a lovely bright azure or with sky blue, according to whether late-flowering gentians or herald-of-heaven (eritrichium nanum) were growing on them. Through the air resonant with the sound of falling water came the sudden whistling of marmots in counterpoint to the cawing of the choughs which circled, remote and elegant, manifesting their indifference to the severity of the heights. On the horizon, beyond rows of green ridges, the white summits of the Isère range were beginning to stand out against the sky, while nearer to hand the snows of the Grand Combin shone above the crests of the Val Ferret. Yet the landscape immediately opposite was growing ever more indistinct in the gathering shade of evening, formless battlements rising behind ill-defined glaciers. Apart from the hut that had been built on the skyline, whose grey and invasive cement I ignored, there remained no trace, no sign of recent human transit. Mountaineers in these parts are like migrant birds: with the end of summer they all leave. In no way dulled by the uphill grind, my spirit was full of wonder, of expectation, of memories, and as in dream everything is jumbled together, strange scenes arose in my mind in which I occupied the centre of the stage.

One after another the stars rose, twinkling brightly despite the diffuse light cast over the mountains by the rising half-moon. A cumulus cloud which had been forming on one summit now thinned out and the moonlight again shone over the whole range. In its cold pallor all distances and proportions were falsified. It was like being in a world of the imagination where anything was possible, populated by blithe spirits and huge phantom beings. The clear

1 The author climbing the steep slopes of Grand Pilier d'Angle

air was full of echoes; swift puffs of wind played follow-my-leader. Absorbed by this magic of opalescent forms I halted, ready to spend the night rolled up in my sleeping-bag behind the shelter of a rock.

The bivouac was a short one, the constraints of the mountain environment compelling me to start out again in the hours before dawn, which are the safest with regard to objective dangers. Thus by four o'clock in the freezing September morning I was already clambering up the mountainside by the feeble light of my head-torch, the moon having set. So I zigzagged up the stony ridge which I had so often ascended and descended in the course of my climbing. The slender ray of light which shone in front of me as I looked for landmarks lent a kind of intimacy to my progress. From the loose moraine I moved on to snow slopes, and then on to weathered rocks which led me up the Col de l'Innominata. It was early. Now growing longer with the end of the summer season, the night was still inky black, so that as soon as I switched off my head-torch I seemed to be swallowed up by the mountain. The first light would not be long in coming, and in the meantime I curled up in my bivouac sack just on the other side of the col, waiting in silence. The stars twinkled brightly above the dark masses of rock around me, and from time to time came a murmur of wind or the heavy thud of a settling ice-tower on the Fresnay Glacier below.

The great rock-fortresses began to grow paler. The Aiguille Noire de Peuterey in particular soared vertically upwards, pitiless, imposing, indifferent to the tiny, fragile human presence at its foot. By the pallid light of dawn I began to clamber down the gloomy, hundred-metre Innominata Gully which

*debouches on to the Fresnay Glacier. On the entire
southern flank of Mont Blanc there is no more
tormented glacier than this one, bristling with
tottering towers of ice and riven with appalling
crevasses. The only safety factor here is the chill of
the early morning, which retards the crumbling of
the seracs, and the sole means of defence for anyone
wanting to cross the glacier is speed. Aware of its
sinister reputation, I reached the beginning of that
labyrinth of collapsing ice and set out to dash across
its conglomeration of creaking ridges, mouldering
spires, rubble and grim chasms waiting to swallow
up whatever falls and send it down into the bowels of
the mountain. Running like a madman I crossed the
glacier in a few minutes. Once out of danger I could
get back my breath while admiring the first rays of
ruddy light on the topmost ridges of Mont Blanc.
Purified by those grandiose surroundings, my mind
entered into intimate communion with the primaeval
mountains.*

*Now the sun had flooded the whole upper basin of
the Fresnay Glacier with dazzling light, but down at
my level a wind had risen, its gusts still cutting with
nocturnal frost.*

*After overcoming a steep ice-slope I climbed on up a
system of rocky corners on the left of the dangerous
ice-gut which descends from the north col of the
Dames Anglaises, thus emerging on to the ridge of
the Aiguille Blanche slightly above the usual point. I
was no newcomer to the spectacular pulpit where I
now stood, but on that day it was as though Mont
Blanc desired to reveal its most hidden mysteries.
Lights, shapes and colours seen from that vantage
point seemed like a veritable apotheosis of the
mountain, both proof and symbol of its dominion, its
magic. And to render the enchantment of the view
still more intense, the great Brenva Glacier now
appeared beneath my feet, stretched out like a
tapestry hanging from the rocky needles of the
summits down to the valley, embroidered with silver
and inset with emerald, opal and aquamarine. Yet
higher above the Brenva the spell was in no way
lessened — here, promontories suspended in space;
there, endless crests whose gesticulating pinnacles
alternated with soft, lyrical curves of snow; and on
all sides overhanging cornices like ocean waves
frozen in the last moment before breaking. There
were proud mouldings of green ice literally plastered
on the vertical walls of rock; immaculate domes and
white peaks sharp as sharks' teeth; vertical-sided
towers, jutting structures of polished red granite;
more pointed summits, and still others crowned with
jumbled blocks all cracked and riven. Most
impressive of all, because nearer, was the Aiguille
Noire, isolated and superb, stabbing the sky with its
colossal point.*

*I was completely absorbed in contemplation of the
surrounding marvels when from the abyss below*

*there suddenly came a tremendous boom like a
prolonged clap of thunder. An avalanche had broken
loose from the icy slopes of the Brenva and was
rushing downwards in a boiling cloud. Knowing the
place and the scale of the phenomenon I shuddered,
following that primordial rite of nature in an ecstatic
trance from my high viewpoint right through to its
end. For several minutes the avalanche continued
tumbling over itself in the shock and thunder of its
ruinous course.*

*At last peace returned, but my eyes continued to
search the deep tangle of seracs, veritable ice-
palaces overhanging the void. Those enormous
masses in delicate balance, the maze of crevasses,
the vertiginous outcroppings, the innumerable snow
bridges suspended above the chasms, the terrifying
echo of rending ice: no more eloquent definition
could have been found for a zone of death.*

*From the high regions where the glaciers originate
comes most of the crumbling debris of the proud
mountains, rubble produced by weathering which
falls downhill and is then carried forward year after
year by the irresistible current of ice. Thus, lower
down in the enormous basin, I could see great
boulders and huge piles of stone and sand sticking
up above the surface. In the course of their slow
voyage they would one day come to a steeper slope or
the sill of a sudden drop where they would all roll
down and lie jumbled together, giving an impression
of catastrophe. Still farther down towards the forest,
where the glaciers had all vanished, appeared vast
morainic formations, wedge-shaped or drawn out
like a shoreline. Those enigmatic witnesses which
had withstood the ravages of time spoke to me of
far-off things and continued to raise questions. It
was as though the ice-age had ended only yesterday.
Peacefully, completely detached from the troubles of
mankind, I stood on my ledge high above the Brenva
Glacier and gazed down at the world like an eagle in
flight.*

*I began to scramble upwards again over easy but
rather loose rocks. Everything I touched moved, and
sometimes a hold would snap off in my hand. This
happened each time I came to a part of the mountain
which had been under snow for a long time and
where the thaw had then exposed the eroded surface.
The midmorning heat had formed a woolly layer of
cloud above the Val d'Aosta which was now
stretching out towards the range of Mont Blanc.
Given the time of year there was nothing to worry
about, but the rapid development of the cloud
nevertheless induced me to increase my pace. Before
long the lower summits had disappeared under the
blanket of fog, which continued to rise until it
reached the glacier below the Col du Géant. Where a
few minutes before the sun had shone in a blue sky,
great waves of vapour were now curling, throwing
cones of shadow on the snow and forming chasms*

through which the sunrays shone like the beams of powerful searchlights.

Continuing its climb towards the higher peaks, the cloud layer presently reached the mountain on which I was climbing. At first it was light and transparent, ravelling out along the crest above me; then, thickening, it obscured the sky, and before I had reached the Punta Gugliermina I was surrounded by swirling, threatening vapour. It grew cold, and small white objects, hard like grains of rice, began to fall through the air in a disorderly sort of way, bouncing off my hands and pattering on my anorak. Suddenly all the pleasure went out of the climb. The mountain had grown hostile, and once again the insignificance and feebleness of man face to face with the forces of nature became apparent.

Luckily, as I had expected, the trouble did not last long. The vapour around me began to thin out, fraying off the rocky needles on which it remained caught, and already caves were opening up in the banks of fog below, showing the reflections of the glacier. The same thing happened on the snowy crest which I was on the point of reaching; the reflection became so strong that it hurt my eyes. I had now attained the altitude of 4,000 metres, and the high southern ridges of Mont Blanc rose above me more imposing than ever. The bare rocks emerged from the snow in huge, elongated forms, endowing the face with the austerity of a gothic stained-glass window. Among these superb structures stood out the Central Pillar of Fresnay where, years ago, I had taken such punishment that it had aged me permanently. The Central Pillar! The memory was enough to bring back yesterday.

I was now on the first of the three snowy points which make up the summit of the Aiguille Blanche de Peuterey. The sky was blue again and was going to stay blue, installed on the summits like something tangible. A scene of colossal grandeur and austere beauty began to open out before me. In front rose the monolithic Grand Pilier d'Angle, or Eckpfeiler Buttress, and on its right the most severe, grandiose and fascinating of all the works of time on the eastern flanks of Mont Blanc, the Brenva Face.

To appreciate the works of nature, like those of art, one has to be at the right viewing point at the right time, or forms, colours and proportions may not be revealed. From the summit of the Aiguille Blanche that day I could look straight into the Brenva Face experiencing it as one who had climbed it many times and from all sides. Indeed, I could make out every detail of its precipitous architecture, whose crazily bulging ice-cliffs apparently suspended from the sky offered prospects of routes still more remote from the measure of man and his limits.

Having crossed the final summit of the Aiguille Blanche, I descended the 150 metres of steep ground which led to the gentle snows of the Col de Peuterey.

2 The tragic bivouac on the Central Pillar of Fresnay, 1961

This is the only flat place on the entire climb, but also the most lonely one, cut off from the world by enormous walls in front and immense drops, ravaged by avalanches, on either side. It was now getting on for noon, and very hot. The softening snow had soaked me up to the knees. A slab of rock stuck out of the col like a monstrous prehistoric head, and I decided to rest on it until the frost should harden the snow again.

Stretched out barefoot in the sun, voluptuously tired, I gazed around drowsily at the surrounding crests on which the snow, struck head-on by the intense light, seemed to glow with an incandescence of its own, forming barriers of inaccessible purity. Over towards the mountains of the Isère a low line of clouds still stained the horizon. A vast silence reigned, a deep peace which gave rise to meditation. I thought of the hours of action I had just been through and those which still lay ahead in my lonely course. It pleases me to seek myself in action and in things; I am even jealous of my spiritual independence. It was for this reason that I had not wanted to share these few days with anybody but rather to experience them in the intimacy of my own emotions, in contact with nature in a familiar and marvellous embodiment, from which I would emerge as from a dream, happy to have dreamed.

Passively drifting in a luminous reverie as the hours went by, I plunged deeper and deeper into a maze of thought which bore me irresistibly towards the ongoing search for my own truth. I felt in myself the tearing contradictions which are part of the human condition, though without succeeding in making any meaning out of the new contrasts to which they gave rise. In my monologue, nevertheless, I reached certain firm conclusions. For example, I was certain

3 Bivouac near the top of the east face of the Grand Pilier d'Angle. Dawn, 12 Oct. 1963

that nothing existed on earth which did not belong to all and thus to me also; I knew that to understand beauty was to possess it; I could swear that doors were always opening in us; I recognized that difficulties did not test man's strength but his weakness. Furthermore, it greatly fascinated me to define a reality as simply the reflection of its idea, though I took it for granted that one lives as one dreams: alone. To other difficult questions that I asked myself, some of which remained unanswered, I found the reply that in the last resort life is given meaning by living it with a maximum of engagement, by seeking to realize all its potential. I understood that I could never have deprived myself of what I thought it right to do, despite all the fear and doubt it had caused me.

I knew that my ideas would sound strange, to say the least, to a certain type of interlocutor. In such a case, however, that would be his problem, not mine. I knew equally that some of my notions were well founded, and I saw more clearly than ever that my eccentricity was perhaps preferable to what passes as popular wisdom. Down there, caught up in a world ruled by custom and the kinds of pressure that succeed in turning even art and faith into merchandise, the apparent calm is one of desperation, a desert of selfishness and apathy. I said to myself that a world where the emotions of fear and enthusiasm only terrify the majority of people, oriented as they are towards sparing themselves and their own feelings, could never be a beautiful one.

By the time I came back to earth from my daydreams the sun was about to set behind the Brouillard Ridge. The air suddenly became cold and the sky turned a fixed, icy grey. I pulled on all my spare clothing, and to while away the time made something hot to eat and

saw to a number of small tasks. Finally I watched the sunset until the last trace of pink faded from the sky. Once there was no more temptation to try to get one last photograph I put the camera back in my rucksack and stretched out happily in my sleeping-bag on the same rock where I had first sat down. The rising moon flooded the sky with a particularly radiant light, preventing the night from growing dark but not from diffusing its infinite calm. In the sharp September frost everything was still, the silence unbroken. The glaciers emitted not the tiniest creak, the river far down in the valley did not murmur, there was not even a whisper of wind. Only the stars moved, a great sea of stars into which one merged. Thus while the cold moon lengthened and withdrew its spectral glimmer on the snow I lay there like an uncertain, fragile statue of ice, breathing the magic of a night which seemed to come from another world. I was drunk with solitude and those imaginings which at times lift us out of ourselves and place us where we would wish to be.

Later, when I stretched my head out of the shelter of my bivouac sack, the moon had set and it was dark and cold. Thus I was unable to carry out my initial project of continuing by moonlight in the early part of the night, but instead I desired to watch the marvel of dawn from the summit of Mont Blanc. It was time to get moving. I crawled out of my sleeping-bag and immediately shivered. The cold was paralysing, but gradually the mind exerted its control over physical suffering and the temperature began to seem more bearable.

The silence was of such intensity that it stunned. I switched on the head-torch and took the first few steps to the col. My crampons rasped on the frozen snow and at times I almost seemed to hear the mountain cry out. I climbed up the snowy rocks of the Grand Pilier d'Angle. Afterwards, on the sharp crest which succeeds them, gusts of wind enveloped me in fine, whirling snow-crystals. Caught in the beam of my head-torch they seemed like stardust. All that now stood between me and the summit was the stupendous ice-ridge which is such a feature of Mont Blanc de Courmayeur, the fore-runner of the main summit. I made short work of this steep, 500-metre bastion, and as I surmounted the cornice I saw on the other side the tiny lights of the still-sleeping villages of Savoy. The faint starshine sufficed to light my way across the wide, gentle slope of dry, floury snow, whose outlines were lost against the sky. Soon afterwards I recognized the summital dome of Mont Blanc, pale, almost spectral, before me.

In the east the sky began to lighten. The dawn wind sprang up, raising clouds of white powder. Gradually the atmosphere became finer, more transparent, in harmony with the increasingly turquoise blue of the sky. The air was utterly pure,

ideral as though it came from another planet. To
breathe it felt as though I were filling my lungs with
sky. The very snow on which I walked seemed
transformed into light and to belong more and more
to the vault of the heavens. One ceased to believe that
it was based on solid material, rooted to the earth.
The rounded ridge on which I was walking became
sharper. I advanced along a crest of ice, and as it
levelled off I found myself on the summit of Mont
Blanc.

I had reached my goal, and suddenly I experienced a
moment of revelation. There was nothing before me
but light and space, immense silent ranges wrapped
in eternal snows. Eastward among them rose the
distinctive shapes of the Matterhorn and Monte
Rosa, dominated in turn by an arch of red vapour
which heralded the sunrise. Under these wavering
summits the long green valleys lay stretched out, still
sombre in darkness. Blowing freely across the slopes
the wind drove frozen under my clothes, but this did
not last long because soon the first ray of sunlight
made its triumphal entry into the white ocean of
silence. What followed belonged more to the
multicolouring of feeling than to that of physical
things. Yet the sun's warm colours did begin to slide
between peaks, faces, ridges and gullies, creating a
kaleidoscopic movement of lights and contrasts.
Nearby cornices took fire from the fine snowdust
suspended in the air, and all around me thousands of
tiny frost crystals lit up the snow. Utterly blue, the
sky remained the greatest thing in the firmament,
embracing distances that tired the sight. Ranges of
mountains overlapped, merged, separated again for
no apparent reason, a myriad points emerged in
confusion, the fine crests contended with their own
shadows for the luminosity of the snowfields, and the
glaciers below seemed like broad lakes of light
cradled between the summits, their surfaces
disturbed by sudden squalls of crevasses. Without
stint, nature was inviting me to a great feast that
nourished my spirit. Thoughts arose from the
perpetual flow of things to the mind and from the
mind to the objective world. I felt new emotions born
in me, unknown dimensions which invariably escape
any attempt to explain them, and which the rational
self sometimes fears to discover. Sunk in that
intimate solitude, the imagination gathered new
impetus. More than ever, I saw with the eyes of the
mind, listened to the great breathing of nature, gave
human proportion to the infinite, grew until I
merged into the universe: I felt all the beauty and the
wonder of existence. At last I had reached truth, the
only possible truth beyond all questioning, the truth
of the heart.

*4 The sun rises from behind the
Matterhorn, bathing the
summit of Mont Blanc in light*

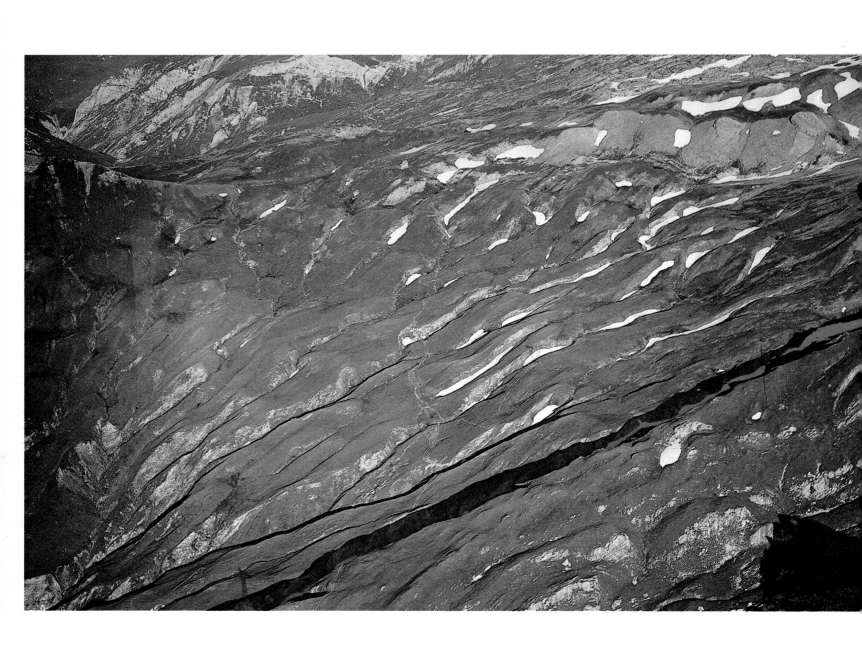

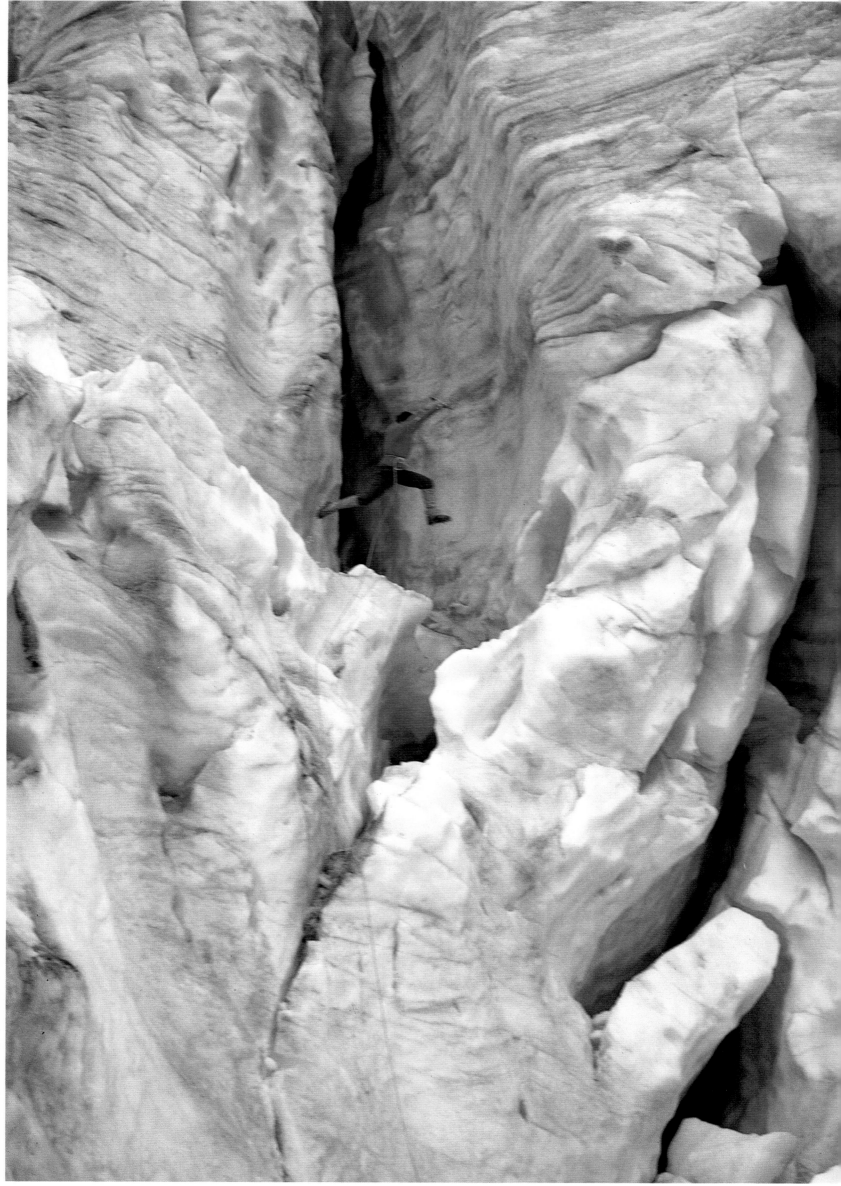

A Note on Photography

The title **Magic of Mont Blanc** *was chosen in order to define the criterion applied in the choice of photographs. What I have sought to bring out especially is the fantastic, almost the abstract, aspect of this mountain — in short, its soul — instead of the more usual technical and historical aspects which, though remarkable in themselves, tend to limit its range of appeal.*

I can say that this series of pictures of summits and glaciers has taken most of my adult life to amass. For the most part they are images of the Mont Blanc that I have explored in the course of my climbs and that I have experienced intensely in good times as in bad.

Especially at first, I did not always possess a high-quality camera, and my supply of film was always limited. I must admit also that in particularly difficult circumstances I sometimes did not have the will to get the camera out of the rucksack. Most of the valley photographs, on the other hand, were taken more recently, when I had better equipment and more experience.

The film used was almost exclusively "Kodachrome II". I preferred this slow film (25 ASA) in order to compensate for the dazzling light of the glaciers. Filters were always necessary, and I often used a polarized one in order to give more contrast to the sky. I usually used a 35mm lens, occasionally going as low as 21mm or as high as 200mm, but never beyond these limits. Except for the night views, all the photographs were taken without camera support.

1 The Aiguilles de Chamonix

2-3 Brocken spectre on the summit ridge of Les Courtes (3856m)

4-5 Winter sunset on the Grands Charmoz and Grépon in the Chamonix Aiguilles

6-7 The Aiguille Noire (3772m), the Aiguille Blanche (4112m) and the Col de Peuterey (3934m) above the Brenva Glacier

8-9 Shadows of giants falling across the glacier

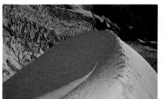

16-17 North face of the Aiguille Blanche de Peuterey: climbers are about half-way up the face, on the ridge leading up to the ice-wall of the hanging glacier

18-19 Warm dawn light on seracs below the Brenva Col at the top of the Old Brenva route

20 On the north face of the Grand Pilier d'Angle

21 On the Whymper Spur of the north face of the Grandes Jorasses, during the first ascent

22 Grandes Jorasses (4208m): climbing the Whymper Spur

23 Cornices on the crest of the Grand Pilier d'Angle, on the Peuterey ridge

24 On the north face of the Grand Pilier d'Angle

25 Finishing out the east face of the Grand Pilier d'Angle

26-27 Light and shadow on the high glaciers of Mont Blanc

28 The Kagami route on the east face of Mont Maudit. In the centre rise the Grandes Jorasses, and along the horizon, l. to r., the Dent Blanche (4357m), Täschhorn

29 Bad weather close to the summit of the Grandes Jorasses

(4490m), Grand Combin (4314m), Matterhorn (4478m) and Monte Rosa (4634m)

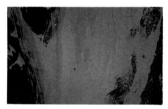

30-31 On the north face of the Grand Pilier d'Angle

33 The north face of Grandes Jorasses: l. to r., Pointe Walker, Pointe Whymper. Along line of light and shadow the north spur of Pointe Croz

34 The north faces of the Aiguille Blanche de Peuterey and the Grand Pilier d'Angle

35 The north faces of the Courtes, Droites, and Verte

38 The precipitous Brenva Face on the Italian side of Mont Blanc

39 The great basin of the Bossons Glacier on the French side of Mont Blanc

40-41 An aerial panorama of the range from the south-west

37 Flying over the Alps in winter. The Mont Blanc range is on the horizon

42-43 A view taken from the edges of Haute-Savoie, showing the chain of summits from the Aiguille Verte on the left to the Dent du Géant on the right

44 The Aiguille du Plan (3673m), one of the Aiguilles de Chamonix

45 The Brenva Glacier with the Aiguille Noire (3772m) towering above it

46-47 The Géant Glacier and the Vallée Blanche. In the background, dominating the Mer de Glace, the Dru, the Aiguille Verte, the Droites and the Courtes

48 Groups of climbers setting off for the Dent du Géant under a windy sky

49 At the top are the Grand Capucin, the Petit Capucin and the Dru, with the Chandelle, Trident and King of Siam below

50 Mont Blanc seen from the rocky ridges of the Brévent

51 Sunset on the Col de Rochefort

52 The Grand Capucin and Mont Blanc

53 Evening light on the Aiguille de Bionnassay

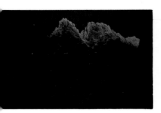

54-55 Last light on the Grands Charmoz and the Grépon

56 The Dent du Géant among the stars

57 The rotation of stars above the Aiguilles de Chamonix, the Dru and the Aiguille Verte

59 The light-trail (across a time-exposure) left by the head-torches of climbers setting out before dawn to climb the Old Brenva route

61 The Rochefort Ridge seen from the summit of the Dent du Géant

63 Storm warning. Dawn light on the snowdrifts of the Col de la Fourche

64 The Mer de Glace. Centre, against the sky, the Tour Ronde (3792m)

65 The two summits of the Dru (3754m)

66 Threatening clouds over Mont Blanc

67 The crenellated crests of the Charmoz-Grépon ridge

68-69 Smoking like volcanoes the summits of the Aiguilles de Chamonix. Sucked upwards by the gale, the snow-plumes rise over 500 metres into the air

70-71 Violent gusts in Val Veni

73 Outliers of the Aiguille du Plan after a snowstorm

74-75 The first avalanches pouring on to the Brenva Glacier after a snowstorm

76 Peaks of the Haute Savoie emerging from a sea of cloud

77 Seracs on the Toula Glacier in winter

78 The Matterhorn from the Col du Géant (telephoto lens)

79 The ice-serpent of the Mer de Glace

80 Mont Blanc from the Dent du Géant

81 Dawn on Col Moore, looking towards the sawtooth ridges of the Val d'Aosta

82-83 The summit of Mont Blanc, a white pyramid 4807 metres above sea-level

84 The ice-fall of the Géant Glacier

85 Early light on the slopes below Col Moore

86-87 The Brenva Glacier opens out like a fan, forming a chaotic ice-fall

88 Seracs in the Brenva ice-fall

89 Crevasses on the upper Brenva Glacier

91 White towers of ice on the Bossons Glacier. In the background, the Dôme du Goûter (4304m)

92 The Requin ice-fall, with the Dent du Géant above

93 Glacier fantasy

94(1)-95(2) Ice avalanches on the Brenva Glacier

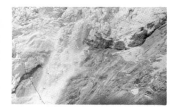

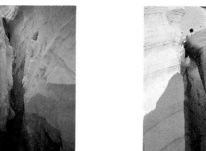

96 Inside a crevasse

97 A snow-bridge over a crevasse

99 Translucencies on the Pré-de-Bar Glacier

100 A glacier caryatid

101 Ice structures, Pré-de-Bar Glacier

102 An ice-monster on the Brenva Glacier

103 The last monster of ice on the Brenva Glacier before reaching the moraine

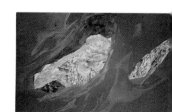

104 The abstract art of an ice-cave

05 Curves and reflections in e glacier hollows

106 Ice-cave at the foot of the Miage Glacier

107 Ice-cave at the foot of the Brenva Glacier

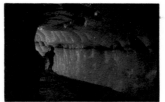

108 During the thaw season a headlong river rushes down this large tunnel which it has carved and shaped along the floor of the glacier

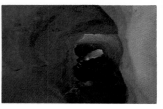

109 A glacier stream, temporarily dried up by the low temperatures of winter, carved out this long tunnel through the ice of the Brenva

16-117 Dwellings on the alp Pré de Pascal opposite the renva Glacier, a scene which as recently vanished, crificed to what is called progress"

118 Alpenrose below the snout of the Lex Blanche Glacier

119 Alpine flowers in the upper Val Veni

120 The last ledges and balconies above the Val Veni

121 Mont Blanc seen between larch trees on the Mont de la Saxe

22 The snout of the Tour lacier and the outlet of its nderground river

123 High waterfall in the Tour cirque

124 The last patches of snow on the southern slopes

125 Chamois

126 Tumultuous waters falling from the Grandes Jorasses into the Val Ferret

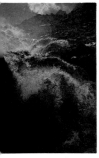

27 The Dora (torrent) di eni bursts out of the Brenva oraines

128 One of the thousands of torrents in the range of Mont Blanc

129 The raging torrent that emerges from the Toula Glacier

130 Marvels of the valley

131 Flowery clearings in the Arve valley

32 The Dora di Ferret

133 The Dora di Ferret during the main period of thaw in early summer

135 Larch wood in Val Ferret

136 Sempervivum

137 Bilberry

138 Little inhabitants of the woods

139 More little inhabitants of the woods

140-141 Colours that are heralds of the glaciers

143 The Bossons Glacier descends between the fir trees of the Arve valley

144 Springtime avalanche near Courmayeur

145 Flying choughs

146-147 Unusual visitors at around 3500m on the Géant Glacier

148-149 View from the summit of Mont Blanc (4807m). On the

left, the ridge forming Mont Maudit, Mont Blanc de Tacul and the Aiguilles du Diable; on the right, the chain of the Grandes Jorasses. In the background are the Pennine alps of the Valais and to their left, hardly projecting, the summits of the Bernese Oberland

150-151 Above the ice-fall of the Bossons Glacier, Mont Maudit reappears after a snowstorm

152-153 Views of the Dent du Géant (4103m) at dawn

154-155 A ray of sunshine briefly lights up the foot of the cloud-wrapped Brenva Face

156 Luminous vapours over the outliers of Mont Blanc. In the background, l. to r., the Triolet, the Mont Dolent and the Aiguille de Leschaux

157 Morning lights and shadows across the ridges from the Triolet to the Dent du Géant

158 Midsummer sunrise over Val Veni

159 First light on the Dent du Géant and the Tour Ronde

160-161 Dawn magic on the Grand Capucin

162-163 The spectral light of full moon falls on Mont Blanc, seen from the Grandes Jorasses

164-165 From the Grand Capucin to the chain of the Aiguille Verte a stormy dawn lights up the mountains

166 Sunset colours on Mont Blanc and the Bossons Glacier after storm

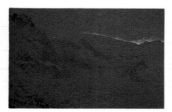
167 The final rays touch Mont Maudit (left) and the Bosses du Dromadaire on the summit ridge of Mont Blanc

168 A cascade of rocky slabs above the Brenva Glacier. In the distance can be seen the Grivola and the Gran Paradiso
169 The Aiguille de la Brenva and the Aiguille Noire de

Peuterey lift their battlemented crests towards Mont Blanc. Seen from this angle, their similar shapes and orientation make them look like projections of each other

174 The summit of the Grandes Jorasses (foreground) seen from that of Mont Blanc. The Pennine Alps in the distance

170 Les Périades of Aiguille de Tacul from Dent du Géant. On the skyline, from left, the Droites, the Courtes, the Tour Noire and the Triolet

171 The Grand Capucin seen from the interior of its bergschrund

172 In the foreground the north face of the Grands Charmoz, with north face of the Grandes Jorasses behind. Centre, the Aiguille de la République

173 The Mer de Glace, the Grandes Jorasses and the Dent du Géant

175 Summits of the Vanoise and the Dauphiné from the Brenva Glacier

176 Huge cornices on the east face of Mont Maudit

177 The Géant Glacier from the Col de la Fourche

178-179 The author on seracs of the Lex Blanche Glacier

180 Roped parties on the rocky needles of Mont Blanc de Tacul

181 On the east face of the Grand Pilier d'Angle

182-183 The east face of the Grand Capucin (3838m)

184 Overcoming the bergschrund at the beginning of the east face of "the Cap"

185 Grand Capucin: the first third of the east face

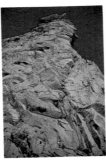

186 Bonatti on the east face of the Grand Capucin in 1976, 25 years after the first ascent

187 Grand Capucin: Bonatti on the upper third of the east face in 1976

188 Climbers at grips with the overhangs of the east face of the Grand Capucin

189 Grand Capucin: climbing the first roof overhang of the east face. On the left is the Trident

190 Grand Capucin: on the east face

191 Grand Capucin, east face: the traverse under the first roof overhang

192 Grand Capucin: climbers on the central part of the east face

193 Towards the middle of the climb

195 The east face of the Grand Capucin. A red bivouac tent can be seen on a ledge just above the middle of the picture

196 Grand Capucin: climbers on the upper part of the east face

197 Grand Capucin:
the final pitches
of the east face

198 Grand Capucin:
Bonatti just below the
summit in 1976

199 Grand Capucin, east
face: the second man
following up the last
pitch

200 A last view of the Grand
Capucin

*Printed in Italy
by Garzanti Editore s.p.a.
september 1984*